YOURS F

Letters from the

Jeff Thorburn has read widely about comparative religions. He became curious about what people believed, and started to write to celebrities several years ago, asking them what they believed. The collection we are publishing is a selection of the replies he has received over the years.

Jeff lives in Warwickshire with his wife and small son.

Yours Faithfully

Letters from the Famous about God

JEFF THORBURN

WITH A FOREWORD BY
ESTHER RANTZEN

Pan Books
London, Sydney and Auckland

First published 1990 by Pan Books Ltd
Cavaye Place, London SW10 9PG

9 8 7 6 5 4 3 2

© Jeff Thorburn 1990

ISBN 0 330 31237 5

Photoset by Parker Typesetting Service, Leicester
Printed and bound in Great Britain by
Richard Clay Ltd, Bungay, Suffolk

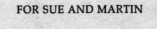

FOR SUE AND MARTIN

CONTENTS

CONTENTS

CONTENTS

FOREWORD
BY
ESTHER RANTZEN

Jeff Thorburn has created a fascinating book. The individual authors are not simply famous, they are gifted and talented, successful, many of them would regard themselves as very lucky. They are the winners, they have walked in sunlight in pleasant places, they have been blessed. You might, therefore, expect them all to believe in God, since He clearly believes in them. But that is not the case; every shade of religious belief is reflected in this book (though not every religion), from orthodox believers to radical doubters. Some of the writers have clearly been inspired by a faith in God, but others believe in humanity, or nature. Some disclaim all belief – as Ned Sherrin puts it, 'I'm afraid I have neither a philosophy of life nor an axiom by which I live. I am Church of England.'

All the same a pattern emerges from this anthology. These are all people who have explored their own beliefs, they have clearly struggled over the years to decide whether life is merely a series of random accidents, or if they are fulfilling a designed destiny. Successful people know their own minds – and many have some good practical advice to pass on. For example, Stephen Fry says, 'In this life one should try everything once except incest and country dancing.' Marc Sinden says, 'Always forgive your enemies, but never forget their names.' And Raymond Briggs warns us, 'Always remember that the light at the end of the tunnel may be an oncoming train.' Clearly the famous people in this collection have had their tough times too, and learned to survive them. The most popular aphorism seems to be 'This above all, to thine own self be true' – perhaps that is the secret of success.

This is a collection of ideas that will surprise you, perhaps inspire you, sometimes make you smile, maybe even cause you to reconsider your own beliefs. My son asked me recently 'Who made God?' I hope he will find the answer in these pages. He will not find one piece of advice I have always treasured, since I first heard it from Terry Wogan, 'As one door shuts, another door closes.' I hope that by reading the book we will all be able to imitate the authors in their success and achievements. Certainly by buying the book, we have the satisfaction of knowing that we are also supporting two immensely worthwhile charities, the National Schizophrenia Fellowship, and MIND.

Esther Rantzen
December 1989

INTRODUCTION

My interest in religion, particularly mysticism, goes back to 1982, and stems from a 'religious experience' I had following an intense period of science study where I found only natural laws or descriptions of reality, rather than a total explanation. It came as some surprise to me, that, once an atheist, I came to believe passionately in God.

Since then I have read comparative religion avidly and have been amazed by the multitude of varying beliefs. I thought it would be enlightening to find out what other people believe in and to see how widely their views differed. I decided to write to distinguished people asking them about their views on God and life, and asked the following specific questions:

a) Do you have a philosophy of life or an idea of God which could be summed up briefly?
b) Do you have a favourite aphorism by which you try to live?

I received many interesting replies from people who were kind enough to share their personal thoughts with me, and finally, after obtaining permission from them, decided to publish the collection as a means of raising funds for two of my favourite charities – The National Schizophrenia Fellowship and MIND.

I hope readers will get as much enjoyment from reading these thoughts as I did.

Joss Ackland

ACTOR

From H. S. Holland, Canon of St Paul's Cathedral, this helped me when my son died:

Death is nothing, nothing at all, for I have only slipped away into the next room. I am I, and you are you. Whatever we were to each other, that we are still. Call me by name, speak in the way you always used. Why should I be out of mind because I am out of sight? I am waiting for you, somewhere very near, and all is well.

For everyday

God give me strength to change the things that need changing, the patience to accept those which cannot be changed and the wisdom to know the difference.

And

This above all: to thine own self be true,
And it must follow, as the night the day,
Thou canst not then be false to any man.

(William Shakespeare, *Hamlet*, Act 1, Scene 3)

John Altman

ACTOR

My idea of God is of an infinite warm bright power which we can only barely touch upon within our basic human souls and minds. We cannot visualize what is at the end of the universe, nor what it would truly be like to confront the full power of God. Love, wisdom and kindness are three clues that we have, here on earth.

One aphorism by which I try to live is: 'Do as you would be done by' which I recall from my childhood reading of *The Water Babies* by Charles Kingsley.

Andy Anderson

ACTOR/SINGER

I have a mind which is usually trying to kill me. As this mind is especially lethal in the morning and waiting for me to wake, I have to make my first action of every day a conscious effort to connect my will and thoughts to that power that runs the universe. This can range from a simple request for help, to be tuned in, to flow with the flow (lead on McDuff), to out-and-out begging for mercy. The latter reaps the best results but can't be manipulated or manufactured by the above mentioned mind – it seems to come from another place entirely and is driven by emotional pain.

Now whether God hears my plea and takes me on board for the day or whether by doing this I surrender enough of my own self-will, rigidity and expectations to allow room for positive gifts and messages to flow, I don't know. What I do know is that my day runs a lot smoother than if I leap up and 'get stuck in' or worse, lie there and try to 'think things through'.

So my belief and experience would be: 'Seek ye first the Kingdom of God . . .'

There are a few prayers and sayings I love and use (and could use more often): The Lord's prayer; The serenity prayer; St Francis of Assisi's 'Make me an instrument of thy peace'. The songs: 'Take my hand precious Lord'; 'For ever young'; and one from the American humorist

[3]

Lord Buckley, 'There is a great power within'. That when used in beauty and immaculate purity can cure – and heal – and cause miracles. When you use it, it spreads like a magic garden and when you do not use it, it recedes from you.

Littlies through the day: Trust God, clean house, help others; Yesterday is history, tomorrow is a mystery – live today; It came to pass – it didn't come to stay.

A roadie from a rock band of mind had a beaut for all the hassles and trials of life on the road – he'd toss in: 'Well, on the cosmic scale . . .' which at the time usually made me more agitated but it did throw a good perspective on things.

If I was to have my own quote, I suppose it would be: 'Hold on and let go'.

Of all the prayers, sincere, wise and beautiful, the most effective for me, and please believe I am not being in any way facetious or sacrilegious here, the most important prayer I ever made came from the bottom of my heart, at a time when I had *no* answers, and this prayer had immediate and life-changing results – the prayer was 'God help me, I'm fucked'.

Jean Anderson

ACTRESS

I am not a good church-goer, but I think we have to have God in our lives.

I don't think it matters if he is called Buddha or Jehovah. The God I feel I can understand best is God the Holy Ghost.

As for a philosophy of life, I feel we should count and give thanks for our blessings and try to learn and come out 'plus' for the tragedies in our lives. I try (not always successfully) to do as I would be done by.

Jeffrey Archer

AUTHOR

My philosophy is quite simply:

> The heights by great men reached and kept
> Were not attained by sudden flight
> But they, while their companions slept,
> Were toiling upward in the night.

Henry Wadsworth Longfellow
The Ladder of Saint Augustine

Paddy Ashdown

POLITICIAN

I do believe in God, but worship him privately. I do not go to church as a result, I suspect, of having too much hate preached at me during a Northern Irish upbringing. My own God is, therefore, not a member of any formal Christian faith but, apart from that, is a fairly conventional one.

I have no particular favourite aphorism. Being an impatient fellow, however, I suspect that if I were to write a book, I would call it 'But at my back I always hear/Time's wingèd chariot hurrying near', an extract from the Andrew Marvell poem 'To his Coy Mistress'.

Eileen Atkins

ACTRESS

My thoughts about God are extremely complicated and change daily. I go back and forth believing everything and nothing. Having seen news footage on the television of drought and famine in the Third World on a Saturday night I get into a fury that the Church of England can sing 'All things Bright and Beautiful' on a Sunday morning. I'm told if I took instruction I would find answers, but what enquiries I have made into the Church of England and Catholic faiths have done nothing to rid me of my doubts or convince me in any way that there is a God . . . and yet . . . and yet . . .

I sometimes feel there is a Force, with a capital 'F', that is there – sometimes I can even call it God. I think probably I'm a pantheist.

As for a maxim – well, there are lots I'd like to live by but know that I don't. All I can say is that if I'm depressed (which is rare) I try to stick to three daily rules that a friend told me once which are:

Each day do:
something for yourself;
something for someone else;
spend ten minutes in prayer or meditation.

Going back to God, I must say that reading the poetry of T. S. Eliot is like having my own vague mystic thoughts that I

EILEEN ATKINS

can't express put in a wonderfully enlightening way – but when I enter the church that he belonged to I feel like saying 'That isn't what I meant at all, Not what I meant at all'.

Sir Alfred Ayer

PHILOSOPHER

I do not believe there is a God. If you count Voltaire's 'Aimer et penser, c'est la véritable vin des esprits' as a philosophy of life, it will serve as mine.

A maxim by which I have tried to live is one given to Bertrand Russell by his grandmother: 'Thou shalt not follow a multitude to do evil'.

George Baker

ACTOR/WRITER

My philosophy of life must be summed up in my idea of God whom I think to be an omnipotent power of love into which man may tap, but seldom does. It is so difficult to watch for one brief hour.

Love your neighbour as yourself. That is quite difficult enough for one lifetime.

Peter Barkworth

ACTOR

I like the Shavian idea of God as life force. God is life. Life, living things, lives to make God manifest. They, the living things, renew themselves; they are not immortal, life is. From trees to humans they are born, grow, mature, decay, die. New ones take their place. I believe in many Christian ideas except anything to do with a 'miraculous' birth and anything to do with the resurrection of the body, or the soul, or any form of life after death.

The Bishop of Durham is right to raise these issues. I do not think Jesus was God/life made manifest any more than any other man. But – of course – I believe he lived. His deification, and that of Mary afterwards, are absurdities which have spoilt it all. Christianity has become a 'tradition' rather than a fact.

Do not tell anybody else what to do. Allow them.

Rosie Barnes

POLITICIAN

I am an atheist. My favourite aphorism is: 'Do unto others as you would be done by'.

Tony Benn

POLITICIAN

The teachings of Jesus, the carpenter of Nazareth, about the brotherhood of man – which embraces men and women equally – have greatly influenced and still influence all our contemporary ideas about liberty, democracy, equality, solidarity and internationalism.

(Extract from *Our Common Humanity*)

Suzanne Bertish

ACTRESS

I believe in God – I believe God exists inside every one of us – and our life's journey, struggle, is in making a true connection with God, opening, listening, feeling, trusting, loving – mankind is out of tune with nature. Mankind is out of tune with man. The collective struggle of life on earth is immense but only through the realization that our journey on earth is singular will man find the courage to turn away from the materialism and look within to the spiritual. Then the power of the collective unconscious could change the world – I believe in man's spirit, man's heart and man's soul – I believe in reincarnation.

My favourite aphorism is:

> This above all: to thine own self be true,
> And it must follow, as the night the day,
> Thou canst not then be false to any man.

(William Shakespeare, *Hamlet*, Act I, Scene 3)

Caroline Blakiston

ACTRESS

Jung said, 'The human psyche strives towards wholeness'.
I strive!

Chay Blyth

YACHTSMAN

I'm sorry to say that I have no 'world view'. I'm quite an ordinary person who likes the quiet, simple things in life.

My only strong view is that you cannot continually take out of life, you have to put something back. I do this via the charity I support.

Chris Bonington

MOUNTAINEER/WRITER/PHOTOGRAPHER

I believe there is some kind of force or power that we cannot explain but I am not at all sure how concerned that force or power is in the fate or doings of mankind. I do believe that we have a responsibility to the society in which we live and that this includes the underprivileged, be they in the Third World or our own country. If people could show kindness and concern, combined with tolerance for the people around them, the world would certainly be a much more comfortable place to live in.

My purpose in living is the joy of discovery and meeting challenges in harmony with the people around me.

Geoff Boycott

CRICKETER

Very sadly I have no specific aphorism or philosophy. Everything I've achieved has been through hard work.

Gyles Brandreth

WRITER/PRESENTER

My favourite aphorism is this: 'When we get up tomorrow morning we may well be able to do without our tragic awareness for an hour or two, but we shall desperately need our sense of the comic'.

Another favourite quotation comes from W. B. Yeats: 'The best lack all conviction, while the worst Are full of passionate intensity'. (*The Second Coming*)

Raymond Briggs

ILLUSTRATOR

Always remember that the light at the end of the tunnel may be an oncoming train.

Sir Edward Du Cann

POLITICIAN

I certainly believe in God and my views are orthodox Christian views. I hope I also subscribe to orthodox Christian values.

I have a dread of aphorisms. I do not believe it is ever possible to say that one orders one's life in accordance with a few attractive phrases; rather one evolves a philosophy, or behavioural patterns, as a result of a mixture of a lifetime's education and experience.

However, if there is a particular saying which has always appealed to me, though I have not invariably practised it with consistent success, it is the Duke of Wellington's advice to complete the business of the day within the day.

Fanny Carby

ACTRESS

I would say one is nearer to God when in harmony with nature and I feel this very strongly sitting at the end of my garden in the country and looking over the Chilterns and watching the old dog fox pad along the field (there is no hunting round my area). Also, when feeding the birds in winter and they come to the table. As I watch them, I experience a great inner peace.

My philosophy of life is to never kill or harm any animal or bird because if you can inflict cruelty on a creature less strong than you and one who is powerless to defend itself, then it is only one step to inflicting the same on a child or a helpless person. Therefore, I do not think this outlook is sentimental but eminently logical – if you cannot stamp on a butterfly you cannot stamp on a baby.

My favourite aphorism is 'Facta non verba', my old school motto – 'Deeds not words'. I am sick of hearing people saying such things as 'They keep that dog chained up all day' or 'I hear that child screaming and there doesn't seem to be anyone there in the day', but, of course, they feel they mustn't intervene. This is to my mind the greatest sin of all – the sin of omission.

Barbara Cartland

NOVELIST

A Prayer

One thing I know, life can never die
Translucent, splendid, flaming like the sun
Only our bodies wither and deny
The life force when our strength is done.

Let me transmit this wonderful fire
Even a little through my heart and mind
Bringing the perfect love we all desire
To those who seek yet blindly cannot find.

We give to the world as much of the life force as can flow uninhibited through our confining bodies. This is our task, the reason we exist, to transmit the Godhead through us. How poorly we succeed and how much more successful we could be!

Leonard Cheshire

EX RAF

You talk about an idea of God. But, of course, it is totally impossible for any human being to be able to picture God. Indeed the clearer the picture the less like him it is. Naturally there are certain things that we know about him because he has revealed them to us, but that is another matter. We know that God is a God of love, but that leaves open a whole question as to what love means in this context. Basically it must mean self giving. There is a continual outpouring of self-giving love between the three persons of the blessed trinity.

Then an aphorism. Inevitably these would change at different stages of one's life and perhaps in response to changing circumstances. I suppose at the moment the one that is most in my mind is: 'Whatever God gives, accept. Whatever He takes, give'.

This came out in a conversation with Mother Theresa a while ago and is something I am trying to follow.

Donald Churchill

WRITER/ACTOR

I believe in God, I suppose, as much as Voltaire did when he said: 'If God did not exist, it would be necessary to invent him.' If you want to believe in God because it gives order and reason to your life and makes sense of the chaos and perhaps some feeling of futility that many thinking people have, then by all means believe.

For myself I think that there is nothing after death as there was nothing before birth.

If I have an aphorism I think that life is *it*, that this life is not a trial run for something else and to believe in any kind of religion less than, say, 6,000 years old – is so unfair, I feel, to the millions who lived and died before then. Why should they be excluded from paradise?

Just get through each day without being a burden on others and if you can amuse them or give them cheer of some kind then you've had a good day.

Arthur C. Clarke

WRITER

See Chapter 'Whatever Gods May Be' in *The Songs of Distant Earth*.

Exploit the inevitable.

Also, 'I don't believe in God, but I'm very interested in him . . . (or her . . .).'

John Cleese

WRITER/ACTOR

I have a very vague philosophy of life. I believe there's some spiritual force that can be contacted if we put ourselves in the right state to do so. I have no idea how it operates and I think we can't be expected to know this – only to be able to experience it if we are lucky.

If you want to know any more, I would recommend a few books: *Lost Christianity* by Jacob Needleman; anything by Maurice Nicol; any of Kenneth Walker's books about Gurdjieff; *In Search of the Miraculous* by Ouspensky. These are all in and around Gurdjieff ideas, which I found the most valuable for me in recent times.

I don't have a favourite aphorism, but my favourite proverb is: 'The tallest trees grow closest to the sky'.

Henry Cooper

BOXER

I am sure that everyone believes in God, which has a civilizing effect and keeps us all sane and separates us from the animals.

You should live every day as it comes and make the most of it and treat people as you would like to be treated yourself.

Jilly Cooper

WRITER

I do not think I have a philosophy of life except I prefer people and animals around me to be as happy as possible, and I want to write as well as possible.

My favourite quotation which I try, and fail, to live by is:

I expect to pass through this world but once; any good thing therefore that I can do, or any kindness that I can show to any fellow-creature, let me do it now; let me not defer or neglect it, for I shall not pass this way again.

(Stephen Grellet 1773–1855)

I do believe in God and I pray like mad when I am in trouble and when I am very happy to say thank you, but I tend to forget about him in between, which is very shabby behaviour.

Paul Copley

ACTOR/WRITER

Ideally I would like to be part of an enlightened society living a life based on personal responsibility, where access to the benefits of a highly developed education system is available on a completely egalitarian basis to all. What I perceive to be personal responsibility, and the moral code to which I try to adhere, are based on my humanist upbringing, and the Christian teachings of the Church and Sunday school of my early youth. Whilst I cannot now pretend to conform to any religion, my sense of right and wrong, of good and evil, are inevitably a result of Christian teaching.

One of my favourite quotations, not by which I try to live but which currently tempers my daily judgements, is: 'A Conservative government is an organized hypocrisy'. (Benjamin Disraeli 17 March 1845)

Michael Craig

ACTOR

I am a complete atheist and find the idea of any kind of god rather touching but absurd – a great deal of wishful thinking.

My favourite aphorism and/or philosophy for life would be: 'Do unto others as you would have them do to you.'

Leslie Crowther

ACTOR/COMEDIAN

Jean and I think the phrase 'God is love' says it all, and 'love thy neighbour' the most important Christian directive. Hard to live up to – but then what's easy?

The enclosed parable also sums up the love of God, and is very inspiring:

Footprints

One night I had a dream.

I dreamed I was walking along the beach with God and across the sky flashed scenes from my life. For each scene I noticed two sets of footprints in the sand, one belonged to me and the other to God.

When the last scene of my life flashed before us I looked back at the footprints in the sand.

I noticed that at times along the path of life there was only one set of footprints.

I also noticed that it happened at the very lowest and saddest times of my life. This really bothered me and I questioned God about it:

'God, You said that once I decided to follow You, You would walk with me all the way, but I noticed that during the most troublesome time in my life there is only one set of footprints. I don't understand why in times when I needed You most, You would leave me.'

God replied, 'Leave you? That was when I carried you.'

Anon

Edwina Currie

POLITICIAN

This above all: to thine own self be true,
And it must follow, as the night the day,
Thou canst not then be false to any man.

(William Shakespeare, *Hamlet*, Act 1, Scene 3)

Non Nobis Solum, Sed Toti Mundo Nati – my old school motto
from Liverpool (Not for ourselves alone, but for the whole
world we were born).

Sharron Davies

FORMER OLYMPIC SWIMMER

I must first explain that although I am, of course, a Christian I am not a well practised or totally convinced one.

My philosophy for life is to try to do unto others as you would have done unto you. I believe that anything worth having has to be worked for and you make your own luck. A little consideration costs nothing. Time, though precious, can be well spent on those a little lonely. Nothing comes easy and laziness is as big an evil as greed. To be successful you must firstly believe in yourself, but not at the cost of others.

Those that work hard generally can afford to play hard, those that aren't prepared to work, or at least try, don't deserve. Be ambitious, but take time to be thankful for what you already have – we have a lot.

Peter Duncan

ACTOR/PRESENTER

I believe in change. Our present cultures are past their peaks and our children will see dramatic events, and their children will only see us as irrelevant history as the way they live will be so different. All gods observe this change and predict its inevitability.

There is no meaning to life except the meaning woman/man gives her/his life, by the unfolding of her/his powers by living productively.

Gwyneth Dunwoody

POLITICIAN

My father, Morgan Phillips, said: 'The Labour Party is more Methodist than Marxist'.

Janet Ellis

ACTRESS/PRESENTER

My philosophy of life is most definitely that 'this is not a rehearsal' and one must seize chances as they arise, lest they're not repeated. I also believe that things you do lay the foundation for what happens – as you sow, so shall you reap; therefore it is worth doing everything to the best of one's ability and to no one's hurt or concern. God seems to me to be a force for good, something I believe exists most powerfully. The Buddhist idea of inner life and central thought comes closest to my personal religious view.

I think my favourite aphorism must be:

> This above all: to thine own self be true,
> And it must follow, as the night the day,
> Thou canst not then be false to any man.

(William Shakespeare, *Hamlet*, Act 1, Scene 3)

Bella Emberg

ACTRESS/COMEDIENNE

Yes, I believe in God who I believe is very broadminded and has a wonderful sense of humour.

Let him without sin cast the first stone

Treat others the same way as you would like to be treated

There but for the grace of God go I.

I try to live by these three. I feel that I am a very poor Christian but I'm still trying to improve. I always think while you live you can have hope.

Lord Ennals

CHAIRMAN UNA AND MIND

I see myself as a very small part of our huge human family, but I am a very privileged part and have two aims: to help improve the lot of the whole of society – especially those who are deprived – and to contribute with them to a greater degree of responsibility for our blessed earth and the environment which sustains it. I have no idea of God but I know that from time to time I am guided to do certain things. That guidance can only come from a supreme life force which I yearn to know better.

D. J. Enright

WRITER

I find the *idea* of God quite fascinating, but am less confident about the *reality*. Never mind that he moves in a mysterious way – but why does He permit so many plain, undeniable, unmysterious horrors?

Sometimes I favour 'Look before you leap', at other times 'He who hesitates is lost'; sometimes 'Many hands make light work', at other times 'Too many cooks spoil the broth'. I would like to live up to the biblical injunction 'Judge not, that ye be not judged', but this is difficult for a book reviewer.

Lady Falkender

POLITICAL COLUMNIST

I do indeed believe in a God – or an energy force for good, which can hopefully keep at bay what seems to be an increasingly powerful energy for evil.

Apart from that, I try to remember the important things in life, and quote to myself the lines of G. K. Chesterton:

> From quiet homes and first beginnings
> Out to the undiscovered ends
> There is nothing worth the joy of living
> But laughter and the love of friends.

Michael Foot

POLITICIAN

I do not subscribe to any religious faith, but I am nevertheless absolutely opposed to the idea of imposing my views on others.

I do believe that everyone should have the right to their own beliefs and the freedom to express them without imposing them on others. (*Methodist Recorder*)

Gretchen Franklin

ACTRESS

There are so many Gods, that I cannot believe in *one* at all. They are all love, I believe, and I hope when I die they will have joined forces and know that I have *tried*.

Of course there is 'love one another', which we all find very difficult, but there's one I always remember – a school master said to my brother: 'You'll cop it up there if you don't behave'.

Stephen Fry

ACTOR/WRITER/COMEDIAN

A 'philosophy of life' seems to me to be an impossible thing for anyone to have. Philosophy is a series of questions, not a system of answers. If you mean 'a philosophy' in the cheap sense of 'do as you would be done by, that's my philosophy', then I don't really have one like that either, but I think that's what you mean by your second question. A theology or interpretation of the meaning or meaningless of existence is a different proposition, and I don't really have one of those either.

I am a rationalist, I believe in logic and the creating power of man above the entropy and chaos of the universe. I certainly have no religious sense of a particular God, although I find the model of the universe presented by many religions to be illuminating and comfortable. Science, after all, is just a theology that makes machines work.

In this life one should try everything once except incest and country dancing. I don't think we need look any further for the perfect ethical code than that, do you?

Sir Vivian Fuchs

DIRECTOR, BRITISH ANTARCTIC SURVEY

To be succinct, I believe the word God represents all the laws of nature, known and unknown, which control our lives and the whole universe. The more we understand, the nearer we are to God.

William Golding

AUTHOR

I have no philosophy of life. My idea of God cannot be 'summed up briefly'. It can be alluded to by the word 'God'.

Of course not. If only life were that simple!

Caroline Goodall

ACTRESS

I have always been taught, and indeed believe, that 'God is the way, the truth and the light'. This is a sufficiently abstract philosophy that can encompass all men and all human aspirations, whatever one's creed or persuasion. The Way, because we are all searching for the right road down which to walk in life; the Truth, because the need for a complete knowledge and understanding of ourselves and others is always in our hearts and minds; the Light, because that is what allows us to live and because it is a metaphor for knowledge.

My favourite aphorism was taught to me by nuns at an early age. Jesus said ask God for anything in my name and it will be given to you. So, somewhat selfishly I ask, 'Dear God, in the name of Jesus, please give/find/help, etc.' for everything from lost pens to major spiritual crises. The success rate is awesome.

Stewart Granger

ACTOR

My philosophy (if you could call it that) has always been never to take myself too seriously and to ride with the punches (there are always punches). Occasionally I throw one but then I'm ashamed, so it's better not to.

Anybody who has a philosophy of life that can be summed up briefly is a phoney. Life is very complicated, my friend.

Lucinda Green

3-DAY EVENT RIDER

I reckon we are all part of a big picture and have not much control over our destiny. When wonderful and dreadful things alike befall us, I believe they must be 'meant'.

I believe that the most destructive weakness anyone can possess is the inability to be truthful, followed by self-pity. There is always someone worse off than ourselves.

You have to sow to reap (you make your own luck).

Sarah Greene

PRESENTER/ACTRESS

A nice aphorism which I like a lot: 'Love makes everything
lovely; hate concentrates itself on the one thing hated'.

Sheila Grier

ACTRESS

I am not a practising Christian or a member of any particular faith. What I do feel, though, is that there is a good spirit around us. If only we weren't so self-centred about individual religions and could learn to love ourselves and others, and be able to give and take more readily without the bigotry of religion and race. It saddens me to see so much destruction of our planet and the human race through ignorance and hatred.

I always try to say to myself, even when things are not going well, that if I really try to believe in it enough 'what's for you won't go by you'.

Susan Hampshire

ACTRESS

You pose a very difficult question to answer briefly but, quite simply, my philosophy for life is hard work and healthy eating (wholefoods).

Sheila Hancock

ACTRESS/DIRECTOR

My philosophy of life really could not be summed up briefly.

I am afraid I don't have an aphorism by which I live.

Max Hastings

EDITOR, *THE DAILY TELEGRAPH*

I am afraid that I don't think my religious convictions would, or should, be of much interest to the general public.

The only aphorism by which I seek to live is that of the Duke of Wellington: 'Always do the business of the day on the day'.

Carol Hawkins

ACTRESS

I do not believe myself to be a religious person but I believe in what is termed as God. I do not see him as a person but as an energy, a power, a creative force which is part of every life form. I am a firm believer in life after death of the physical body. I cannot accept that we are born into this life, go through the experiences and learning processes, only to get old, die and that's the end of it. There must be a purpose for our existence other than what we consciously know of.

I look upon my time here as a learning process, to see myself, to understand others and learn to respect all life forms, including the planet we live on.

I believe that when our physical body dies our spirit lives on in a different dimension according to our state of progress. By progress, I don't mean being a do-gooder, religious or clever, but the way in which we lead our lives, thinking of others, learning from our experiences and trying to help those around us.

It is so easy to judge others but as we all come from the same source, God, and are at different stages of development, how can we judge when we ourselves may have been the same at one time or another. It is very easy to say but can be difficult to put into practice.

This is a very brief outline of what I feel about God and life. One thing is for sure, when I die I'll know one way or the other if my beliefs are true.

[57]

Philip Hayton

REPORTER/PRESENTER

I believe in God. I have no choice. I couldn't believe in man; I couldn't believe in nothing. My faith is simple but deep. The presence of God inspires, assures and comforts me.

It is the foundation of my life. My vision of God and his purpose for us is often faint and I look forward to the day when it all becomes clear.

'Man's search should exceed his grasp, or what's a heaven for?'

Paul Heiney

WRITER/BROADCASTER

Nature knows best.
   Never board a ship without an onion.

Jimmy Hill

PRESENTER

Briefly, I do believe in a superior being but I don't think he wears any particular religious colours.

'Do unto others as you would be done to.'

David Icke

PRESENTER

I am an environmental campaigner, a member of the Green Party and convinced that our way of life in the developed or, I believe, overdeveloped countries is killing the planet and the life support systems that we need to maintain life on earth.

Given that background, I have countless philosophies of life which I try desperately, fighting against temptation and human nature, to live by. It is not easy being perfect, as they say, and of course no one is, but if we don't think more of the consequences of the way we live for future generations, then there will eventually be no future generations.

God is a problem for me . . . I desperately want to believe there is a power for good and the older I get and the more I see the complex web of life that is the world we live in, the more I am moved to believe that there must be a powerful force at work somewhere. But I am not going to say I have total faith in the existence of a biblical God as such because I am yet to have that faith. However, I am moving that way and I want to believe it is true. It would give far greater meaning to life.

My philosophy of life can be summed up in two sayings: We do not inherit the earth from our ancestors, we borrow it from our children. And something that Gandhi said: 'The earth provides for everyone's need but not for everyone's greed'.

DAVID ICKE

We must live more simply so that others may simply live. And: when you have cut down the last tree and polluted the last river, you will know you cannot eat money.

Jon Iles

ACTOR

If I have any philosophy it is to go about my life and work causing the least amount of distress or disruption to the greatest number of people whilst still remaining a strong and entertaining(?) person. (It's not always possible.) I don't have a clear idea of God, I'm afraid. I believe we are in control and distressingly exercise that control with a singular lack of expertise and sensitivity. But we can learn. I wish I did have a clear idea of God – I might sleep better.

Any aphorism I might adhere to has to be along the lines of: 'Don't frighten the horses' and, more importantly, 'Don't hurt them'.

Tony Jacklin

PROFESSIONAL GOLFER

I suppose my philosophy of life is to work hard and tell the truth. The aphorism by which I live is, I suppose, 'To thine own self be true'.

It's so easy in this crazy world to get things mixed up. I see people do it all the time. I try to judge myself as others may judge me; it's not easy.

It's certainly impossible to please everybody so you do as you see fit. If you come out the other end liking yourself, then you're a success.

Joyce Jacobs

ACTRESS

To me, God represents a power for good, and the teachings of Christ, if *really* followed, could only produce a more peaceful world. What some people do in the *name* of religion is a different matter entirely.

My philosophy – The family first and never lose touch. Respect the elderly and never ridicule a person's faith. Be kind.

Derek Jameson

BROADCASTER

I was never baptized, having been born a waif in the East End, but I have a personal philosophy based on the premise that people basically are good.

All my life I have believed that we should always hope for the best, but expect the worst. That way nobody gets disappointed.

Louise Jameson

ACTRESS

There is a seventeenth-century nun's prayer which you probably know. The last sentence reads: 'Give me the ability to see good things in unexpected places, and talents in unexpected people. And, give me, O Lord, the grace to tell them so.'

The other phrase I would like to quote you comes from the man I am going to marry. He is a beautiful artist, oils and water colour. We were discussing ambition one day and I asked him his. After great thought he replied: 'I would like to feed the cat and empty the rubbish with as much care and devotion as I paint a picture.'

These two quotes are really the essence of Buddhist philosophy as I understand it. If we could just *take care* of ourselves, our surroundings, our loved ones. I would like to throw a ball in order for the next person to catch it, not to score a point and win a competition.

Peter Jay

WRITER/BROADCASTER

The only idea of God which I have is that, if there were such a person, he/she would have to be quite extraordinarily malicious and/or incompetent.

My philosophy of life is utilitarian, by which I mean 'the greatest happiness of the greatest number', sensitively interpreted, is the highest good and all other moral maxims either flow from it or must give way to it.

Howard Keel

ACTOR/SINGER

Play young – work old and 'What 50 said' by poet Robert Frost.

'Blood is thicker than water' was invented by undeserving relatives.

Chris Kelly

WRITER/PRODUCER/PRESENTER

I think it never occurs to you that you have anything as grand as a philosophy of life until someone enquires. Since you ask, I suppose I have. If I had to put it in a few words, it would simply go: be kind where you can. I believe the teaching of Christ is without question the most satisfying guide for living. It may not be logical, or practical in terms of career, or fashionable, but it seems to me to make the most perfect sense. Kindness is at the heart of it; sadly it appears to be in short supply.

I haven't got a favourite aphorism but some years ago I promised myself that I would never, ever, make the excuse 'I haven't got time'. It has had a magical effect. I now make better use of what there is.

Felicity Kendal

ACTRESS

Try to treat others as you would like to be treated, and go on from there.

Ludovic Kennedy

WRITER/BROADCASTER

God is an idea in the mind. Some people think he exists outside the mind as well. I do not.

Do unto others as you would be done by.

Bruce Kent

HON. VICE-PRESIDENT CND

I often think of the inscription on Winifred Holtby's grave-stone in Rudstone, Yorkshire:

> God give me work
> Till my life shall end
> And life
> Till my work is done.

God I see as the source of all wonder, love, joy and beauty who cares for all his creation. Yet he cares for us.

Psalm 8: 'When I see the heavens, the work of your hands, the moon and the stars which you arranged, what is man that you should keep him in mind, mortal man that you care for him?'

Neil Kinnock

POLITICIAN

I respect faith in God and the inspiration and comfort which I know that it gives, and believe in the existence of the soul and in the power of redemption.

But despite many hours of thought and discussion with friends who are believers I have never been able to share their conviction.

I readily embrace the values of Christianity and try to uphold them as my own code for living and my own standards for relationships, but like others – including some regular Christian worshippers – I have not been able to commit myself to a degree of belief which requires *faith* in divine design or judgement.

Michael Kitchen

ACTOR

God is the substance of me; the quiddity of me; in the middle, at the beginning to the ends of me; the magic and the power of me; there in spite of me; there in all, living or otherwise, acknowledged or not; there in the race and for many, perhaps most, whose eyes lack the thought, too vast and too simple to see.

Be still and know.

Maxine Klibingaitis

ACTRESS

As a practising member of the Lutheran church I have a strong belief in the Christian faith and would be more than happy to share my thoughts with you.

I can't think of any specific words that encapsulate the gentle greatness of God, or God's universal-size love. God is love. I love God and God loves me and that makes me happy.

The best and most beautiful things in this world cannot be seen or even touched, they must be felt within the heart.

Larry Lamb

NEWSPAPER EDITOR

In so far as I have a philosophy at all, it is a fairly common-place one. I tend to take the view that it doesn't much matter what one does, provided that no one gets hurt in the process. Hurting people, it seems to me, is the only real offence.

I am a genuine agnostic on religious matters. If, how-ever, there is a God, I would like to feel that he thought the same way.

Diana Lamplugh

FOUNDER OF THE SUZY LAMPLUGH TRUST

'God works through people – we are all he has got,' said the new 'trendy' vicar on the BBC's *The Archers* serial of country folk. Well, I have no idea if he is working through me – all I am sure of is that I seem to have been given no choice, no options, and amazingly I am trained to undertake the work which has been thrust upon me. Since realizing that there was a problem of aggression and violence for so many people in their working lives, I feel I have a mission to do all I can to help diminish what has now been acknowledged as a growing concern.

My daughter Suzy left me with an example which I have kept before me ever since she disappeared, eventually presumed murdered, that bright July day in the middle of a normal working Monday.

'Life is for living, Mum,' she admonished me, when I tentatively enquired a few days before whether she was overdoing things. 'We've only got one life and we need to live it to the full,' she went on. She had a wonderful life, she enjoyed her work, her recreation, was fit and healthy, loved and was loved in return. Had she had time to look back on her life she would have had few regrets.

But for months after she had been, as it were, erased out of our lives by a rubber, I was surrounded by friends, acquaintances, the media and those who merely looked on. Many of these counselled, cautioned, cajoled or demanded that I cease to partake in living and instead discreetly mourn in private; stop embarrassing those who wished not to be reminded of a potential threat; be dressed in black and frozen in time. Even the church offered me 'Peace' as though that state was preferable to my determination to be alive and use the adrenalin which accompanies such trauma in setting up a Trust and pursuing its work.

Suzy's disappearance felt like Omega, the end, to us, and the quotation from T. S. Elliot 'In the end is the beginning' became the Trust motto. It is no surprise that all our projects are known as The Alphas.

As I thought about this book I walked around Plymouth with our son who is studying marine sciences. It was a beautiful day and we crossed over the Plym by ferry to Edgcumbe. We were amazed by the glorious castle resurrected from the ashes of a direct hit from a wartime incendiary bomb. The quay clock held a message: 'If you love life – do not squander time.' Well, I reflected, this leisure was well spent, this life continued to be enchanting and challenging.

On the way back, the newly built Plymouth Dome reinforced another belief: 'There must be a beginning of any great matter, but the continuing unto the end until it is thoroughly finished yields the true glory' was the quotation from Sir Francis Drake which spans the entrance hall. Yes, we were doing just that. Dedication, concentration, and sheer hard graft has begun to pay off. Our plans with the Trust have begun to work out.

But still, somehow, I felt that maybe God, alongside all those seen and unseen critics and advisers, disapproved of my stand, my continuing curiosity and excitement in ideas; my action and refusal to 'take a low profile'. And then I came across a Nun's prayer which spoke of 'Peace' as an *active* participation in life' and I understood. I had seen Peace as a negative, or at most a contentedness with the status quo; an absence of emotion, an omega.

I believe Kahlil Gibran when he wrote in *The Prophet*

> Your children are not your children
> They are the sons and daughters of Life's
>   longing for itself,
> And though they are with you yet they
>   belong not to you.

Our lives were enhanced by our daughter, Suzy; she was a blessing with which we were entrusted. None of our feelings about her were diminished by her death.

The life we continue to lead is also entrusted to us to use in the best way we are able. Peace, as I have found it, is quite definitely a positive emotion. Indeed, the whole of living, as I perceive it, is a positive – an Alpha project in itself.

Philip Latham

ACTOR

I'm afraid my philosophy is a movable feast, but a simple statement from Alan Paton's 'Meditation for a Young Boy Confirmed' has stuck in my mind since I read it – possibly because I am constantly slipping off 'The stones' or 'The planks'!!

You will observe that virgins do not bear children, and that
  dead men are not resurrected;
You will read in the newspapers of wars and disasters. But
  they will report miracles with impatience.
You will not wish to disappoint your parents.
You will suffer deep troubling of the soul.
You will cry out like David before you, My God, My God,
  why has Thou forsaken me?
Do not hastily concede this territory, do not retreat
  immediately.
Pass over the slender bridges, pick your road quickly
  through the marshes.
Observe the frail planks left by your predecessors,
The stones gained only by leaping.
Press on to the higher ground. To the great hills and the
  mountains.
From whose heights men survey the eternal country and
  the city that has no need of moon or sun.

Bernard Levin

JOURNALIST/AUTHOR

I suppose I could say that I do not believe that either the universe or our lives are random or meaningless, but that there is some principle which governs both and makes us part of it. If we have any duty, it is to understand this and learn from it what is required of us if we wish to approach full understanding.

Roger Lloyd Pack

ACTOR

I imagine God as an external and internal force, or energy, which is in and out of all things, an untouchable and unknowable presence or spirit. You could say, I suppose that God is Love.

With regard to aphorisms, there are several knocking around at different times that I usually find relevant, but I take particular comfort from 'Sufficient unto the day is the evil thereof' and attempt to live in the moment of today as much as I can.

Ray Lonnen

ACTOR

I don't have a favourite aphorism or philosophy of life except that I see God as the power of good over evil and I try to live by that, inasmuch as I try to be helpful, pleasant and kind to my fellow human beings. In these stressful times, it requires a lot of patience but I do try to keep it in mind.

Barbara Lott

ACTRESS

My basic philosophy of life is based on the prayer by Reinhold Niebuhr: 'God grant me the serenity to accept the things I cannot change, the courage to change the things I can and the wisdom to know the difference.'

William Lucas

ACTOR

Where do the characters in a book come from, why are they there, where are they going? The author invented them, gave them life in order to tell his story, test his truths. They don't see him, they can't, neither do they need to, but he sees them. They are real to him and to one another. Each character is a mixture of various ingredients. As the characters are finished with those ingredients they are redistributed to other characters, each one a new and unique mix. Nobody really disappears, they are redistributed. We exist in one another and in God, for that is who the supreme author is. How his book will end, God knows.

Patrick MacNee

ACTOR

Buddha, Allah, Brahma, Jesus
Or whatever name does please us
Show us good instead of evil
In our strife 'gainst life's upheaval.
And on those days we feel aggrieved
Remind us if another's peeved
And let courage displace worry
That with truth we first say 'sorry'.

Marie Cameron

Revenge retards remission.

Arthur Marshall

JOURNALIST/AUTHOR

My view of God is that if he exists, he is a rotten evil old man.

'Do unto others . . .'

Cliff Michelmore

COMMENTATOR/PRESENTER

It is a great gift, and I do not possess it, to be able to encapsulate in a few words one's 'idea of God'. It is an equal gift, to be able to state one's philosophy of life in a sentence. If I were to try I would assuredly fail, so I will not try.

As for maxims, mottoes and aphorisms, I always think that the daily apples which keep the doctor away this week will give me the stomach ache which will have me in his surgery the next. Put not your trust in the panacea of the aphorism is my guide.

Dudley Moore

ACTOR

Unfortunately, or fortunately – I'm not sure which – there is a philosophy of life that has accumulated around me as I have become more comfortable. The questions of life are not asked when a man is satisfied in his soul, which means first being satisfied socially and economically. I'm afraid that these are 'crass' reasons for feeling OK with oneself, but it's at least an indication of some plateau of calm that is to be reached before some other introverted enquiry begins.

I don't really have a favourite aphorism by which I live. But I do want to enjoy myself as much as possible on earth whatever that means. Be aware of the pain that is implicit in life but don't allow it to rule.

I'm sure my opinions will change as the years go by and organs become defunct.

Desmond Morris

AUTHOR

This is the afterlife.
Each year is more important than the next.

Malcolm Muggeridge

AUTHOR

For the devil is a gentleman, and doesn't keep his word.
(G. K. Chesterton)
 'Thy will be done' – the Lord's Prayer.

Len Murray

TRADES UNION LEADER

God is Love.

Thou shalt love the Lord thy God with all thy heart . . .
and thy neighbour as thyself.

Barry Norman

WRITER/PRESENTER

Yes, I do have an (often shaky) belief in God and a philosophy which I suppose could best be summed up, rather cornily perhaps, in the advice of Polonius: 'This above all to thine own self be true . . .'

Richard O'Brien

ACTOR

I believe that man created God for the purpose of controlling relatively primitive tribes, as well as the kings (soldiers who got lucky) who ruled them. The story of the creation and the Garden of Eden was a way of explaining a beginning to a people who knew only desert wandering – the apple represented knowledge or conscious thought and the serpent stood for the animal within us all. However, I believe that if enough people say that a thing is so, then it can become so, the power of prayer being enormous. This 'wish' at the moment of death must be even more forceful, consequently I believe that there is a cloud of spiritual energy that grows stronger minute by minute as the dying release their souls and go to join it. It is this communion of souls that has become 'God'.

Don't talk about it, do it.

Brian Oulton

ACTOR/WRITER/DIRECTOR

God is spirit and must be worshipped in spirit and truth.
  Perfect love casteth out fear.

Frank Page

JOURNALIST/BROADCASTER

My philosophy is epitomized in the aphorism: Ripeness is all (Shakespeare, *King Lear*, Act V, Scene 2).

Gwen Plumb

ACTRESS

To me God is the power of goodness in the world. I'm not a church-goer but a lover of the outdoors, where I feel closest to God in the flowers and the animals around me.

The word by which I try to live my life is *give*, of myself, my time, warmth, personality, humour.

Magnus Pyke

SCIENTIST

The chief end of man, says the catechism, is to glorify and enjoy God. Now that it can be seen that we have it in our power to provide our material wants by the judicious application of those aspects of science and technology, we can readily agree with the implication of the catechism that the chief end of man is a moral one.

> The young man of Moldavia
> Who did not believe in a saviour
> But invented instead
> With himself as the head
> A system of moral behaviour.

From *Scientific Understanding and the Chief End of Man*
(2/9/65)

Robin Ray

WRITER/PRESENTER

Deliberate cruelty is the one unforgivable sin. (Tennessee Williams, *A Streetcar named Desire*)

If the stone falls on the egg, alas for the egg. If the egg falls on the stone, alas for the egg. (Chinese proverb)

Claire Rayner

JOURNALIST/AGONY AUNT/AUTHOR

Heavens, what a lot to ask for in just one short letter! I think to expect anyone to express a 'philosophy of life' or an 'idea of God' in a brief summary is unreasonable. I'm sorry but I really don't think I can help you with this.

I can do a bit better with your aphorism – there's an old Chinese proverb that says 'This too will pass' and it's one to be applied at all times – good ones, bad ones, interesting ones and boring ones. It gives you a sense of proportion.

William Roache

God is the great creator and beyond our comprehension. But we can, by effort, understand the laws by which we should live in order to get nearer to understanding the absolute Deity.

Always try to improve myself.

Robert Robinson

COMMENTATOR

No.
   'Whereof we may speak, thereof we may speak clearly; whereof one cannot speak, thereon one must remain silent.' (L. Wittgenstein)

Robert Runcie

ARCHBISHOP OF CANTERBURY

A summary of my philosophy of life would be one which sees a human being as the object of God's creative love. Such a view sees life as a grateful response.

My favourite aphorism is 'A Christian is a person who carries about him a sense of indebtedness.'

Pamela Salem

ACTRESS

I believe God created me and that he is a God of love. It follows therefore that if he loves me, then he totally understands me, and the reasons I do what I do, even when I don't understand them myself. It's a good feeling not having to justify or explain myself to Him, but a bit unnerving when I try to stick my head in the sand.

I have two favourite aphorisms:

My father's: 'A little bit of everything and not too much of anything' as a recipe for a happy and healthy life, but it's advice that is quite hard to achieve.

My mother's: 'The day they stop talking about you go out and shoot yourself', which has frequently been of comfort to me when I have been upset by what someone has said.

Brough Scott

SPORTS PRESENTER/JOURNALIST

I do believe in a simple phrase for ordinary life. That is: 'Work hard, enjoy yourself, but care for other people.'

Harry Secombe

ACTOR, COMEDIAN AND SINGER

I have never been one to delve too deeply into 'the meaning of life' but try to live by the Christian ethic of taking one day at a time and am a firm believer in 'live and let live'.

Ned Sherrin

FILM, THEATRE, TELEVISION PRODUCER/DIRECTOR/WRITER

I'm afraid I have neither a philosophy of life nor an axiom by which I live. I am Church of England.

Clive Sinclair

CHAIRMAN, SINCLAIR RESEARCH LTD

No. I do not believe in God.

I follow Kipling's edict in treating the two imposters triumph and disaster both the same.

Donald Sinden

ACTOR

I only have one tenet by which I live – to try to leave this world a slightly better place than I found it.

Jeremy Sinden

ACTOR

I believe that God is 'within' – I believe in God – and I believe that we all worship the same God regardless of the name we give Him. I was brought up to try to leave the world a better place than I found it and to do as you would be done by.

Marc Sinden

ACTOR

To me, God is an all-seeing, all-forgiving being, who allows us to live our lives as we choose, in the knowledge that his security and house will always be there, when we eventually realize how very important they really are.

Always forgive your enemies, but never forget their names.

Cyril Smith

POLITICIAN

I see God as a spirit which inspires emotions and attitudes.
   I try to live on the basis of 'Do unto others as you would
be done by'.

Victor Spinetti

ACTOR

I try to live by my own aphorism: '*Hell* is what you can make of your life. *Heaven* is how alive you can be.'

Ronnie Stevens

ACTOR/DIRECTOR

Life is an attitude of mind.
   Rise above it.

Alastair Stewart

NEWSCASTER

I was born into the Christian tradition and educated by the Roman Catholics.

My philosophy is based on the belief in honesty, fairness and affection.

I suppose the cliché 'Do as you would be done by' is as good as any.

Suzanne Stuart

The most important focus for me is: 'To see the essence of God in *everyone*.'

Benedict Taylor

ACTOR

God is the word given to the force which binds the planet and the universe together. Christians, Jews, Buddhists, Hindus, Muslims, Aborigines, North American Indians, South American Indians, all societies ancient and modern have felt or glimpsed this force and have tried to make sense of it through the limiting tool of language. At our best we're enlightened by it; at our worst we bicker over the semantics of our attempts to label it. We should stop worrying about it, stop fighting over it and get on with feeling it.

If I have any other philosophy, it's to cherish every moment I live and be true to myself, my family and my friends.

Frederick Treves

ACTOR

All humanity seems to me to require some spiritual framework within which it may live. It may be good or it may be
evil, the requirement remains. Why this is so remains a
mystery. Reason tells us the mystery exists, so, from a
reasonable point of view, I must accept the mystery. I
believe in Christ's mystery and without accepting it, could
not live.

My family motto on our coat of arms is my favourite
aphorism: 'Veritas via vite'.

Robert Trotter

ACTOR

It seems to me that a major impulse in becoming an actor is to seek a fullness and completeness (lacking in oneself) in the carefully constructed framework of a fictional character. Into that already (but only partly) existing entity, one can infuse all of one's own inchoate love, anger, doubt, frustration, happiness, compress and contain it and, together with the original creator (the writer), project a powerful image of completeness to a (hopefully) waiting world. Of course, the process of cooperation goes a stage further, in that one normally combines with other actors to project the totality of the writer's blueprint. And as a bonus – one which every actor must hope to attain – that waiting world will become, on however small a scale, a happier place as a result.

That is really all an actor can hope to do, and that – as actor – is his purpose in life. And maybe in a way it's the same for everyone: through a union with others, in a relationship of love and mutual trust (is there divinity there? Yes, perhaps . . .) to make the world, that little bit of it around one, a happier place.

Born an only child, I have always loved the idea of brother – and sisterhood. And as a Scot I turn naturally to my beloved bard Robert Burns for the aphorism (more of a hope really) which sustains me:

For a' that, and a' that
It's comin' yet for a' that
That man to man, the world o'er
Shall brothers be for a' that.

'For a' that and a' that'

Sam Wanamaker

ACTOR/DIRECTOR/PRODUCER

We are such stuff
As dreams are made on, and our little life
Is rounded with a sleep.

(William Shakespeare, *The Tempest*, Act IV, Scene 1)

I do not believe in an afterlife, nor wish for one. What happiness and fulfilment we have is here and now. I am an agnostic.

What a piece of work is a man! How noble in reason!
how infinite in faculty! in form, in moving, how
express and admirable! in action how like an angel!
in apprehension how like a god! the beauty of the
world!
the paragon of animals!

(William Shakespeare, *Hamlet*, Act II, Scene 2)

Fatima Whitbread

OLYMPIC ATHLETE

In relation to my competitive athletics programme I accept that I will win if God deems it so but if I do not He has decided that it was not to be. I fully accept this philosophy and it has helped me to live with victory and defeat.

I attempt to treat people who approach me in the street during my everyday life in the manner I would wish them to treat me.

Desmond Wilcox

TV PRODUCER/JOURNALIST/AUTHOR

I have only the vaguest idea of God but a firm idea of goodness which I believe to be family centred and best encouraged by directing our efforts to the future of our children and the care of the disadvantaged in our community.

Be kind to others while you are on the way up because you will surely meet them on the way down, and I did!

Shirley Williams

POLITICIAN

I am a Roman Catholic and as such broadly accept the Christian doctrine, though I am critical of my church in some respects, especially its view of the role of women. I am persuaded that much of the teaching of Christ makes much sense in our troubled and chaotic world, and I fundamentally believe in the doctrine of the resurrection and of salvation.

As for favourite aphorisms, one would be 'Take what you want, says God. Take it and pay for it.' I believe that those who follow purely worldly success or ambition often find it a very hollow achievement; and the second is a saying from the Bible by St Thomas: 'Lord I believe, help Thou my unbelief', which seems to be very appropriate to our times.

Simon Williams

ACTOR

I believe in God and in love and in the difficulty of believing. Nothing that good is easy.

'It's not a question of good manners or bad manners but that you treat everyone the same.' – George Bernard Shaw.

Norman Wisdom

ACTOR

I can't help you very much since I am neither a particularly philosophical nor religious person, although that doesn't mean I'm an atheist. However, I have one handy aphorism and that is 'There's no fun like work'.

Ernie Wise

COMEDIAN

I believe that if you live by the ten commandments in the Bible you will live a good life.

Mike Yarwood

COMEDIAN/IMPRESSIONIST

I believe that God is present and can be found in those we love.

This is life . . . it is not a rehearsal.

Jeff Thorburn

My answers to my own questions:

God made man like his maker. Like God did God make man. (Genesis 1.27)

Love God and do as you like. (St Augustine)